THE MARGARET THATCHER COLOURING BOOK

BY
NATHAN BRENVILLE

THE
COMPLETELY INACCURATE
ILLUSTRATED BIOGRAPHY
OF
MARGARET THATCHER
FOR PEOPLE
WHO LIKE
COLOURING
THINGS
IN

\Bᵇ\
Biteback Publishing

First published in Great Britain in 2016 by
Biteback Publishing Ltd
Westminster Tower
3 Albert Embankment
London SE1 7SP
Copyright © Nathan Brenville 2016

ISBN 978-1-78590-099-0

10 9 8 7 6 5 4 3 2 1

A CIP catalogue record for this book is available from the British Library.

Layout by Adrian McLaughlin

Printed and bound in Great Britain by
CPI Group (UK) Ltd, Croydon CR0 4YY

MIX
Paper from
responsible sources
FSC   FSC® C013604
www.fsc.org

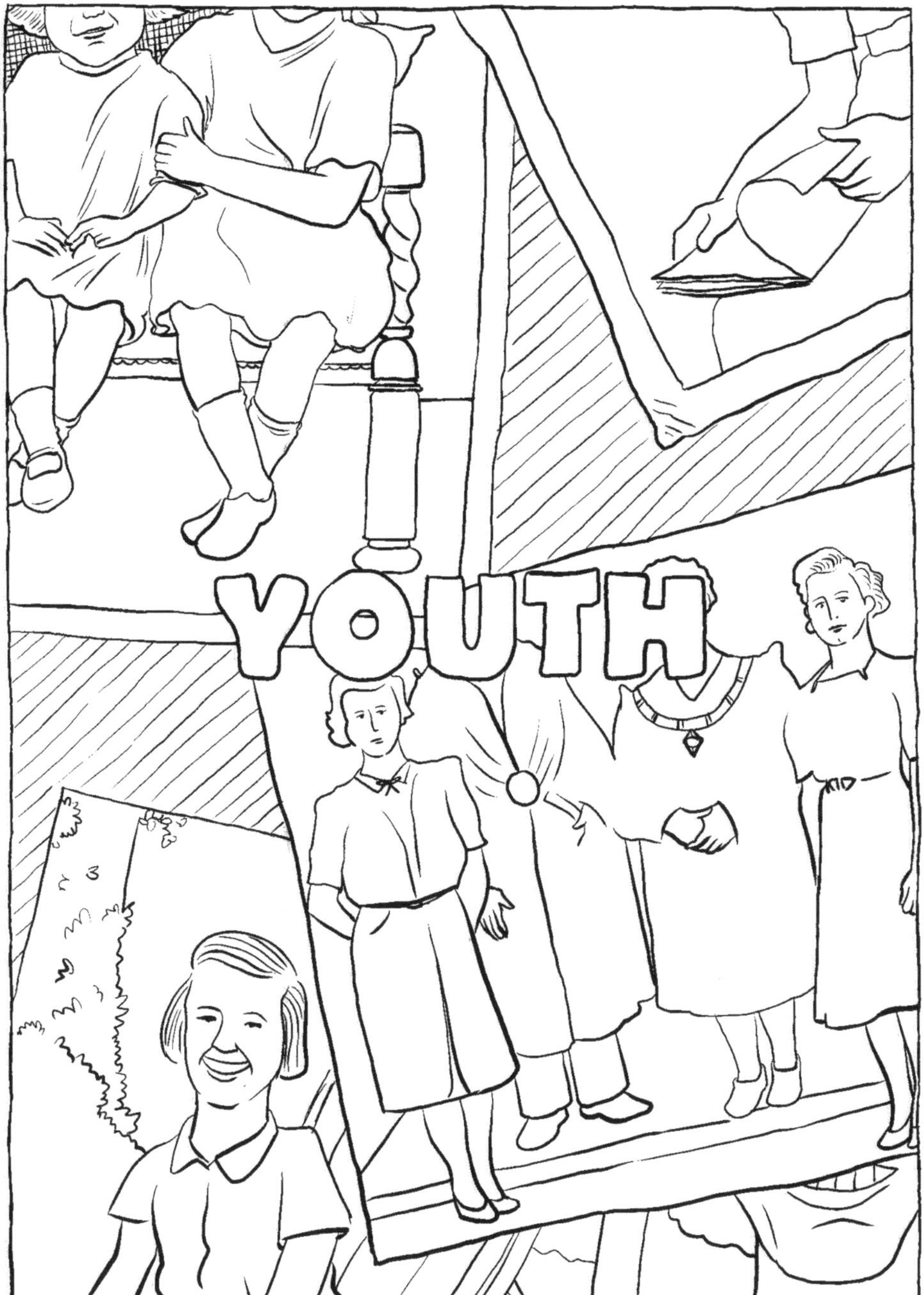
YOUTH

MARGARET ROBERTS INITIALLY SHOWED NO INTEREST IN POLITICS

INSTEAD, SHE PONDERED NEWTON'S THEORY OF GRAVITY

BUT BY SCHOOL AGE SHE'D BEGUN TO THINK OF THE FUTURE

IN 1935, MARGARET JOINED HER FIRST CABINET

AS A TEENAGER, MARGARET HAD A STEADY JOB WORKING
FOR RONNIE BARKER, BUT SHE DREAMED OF GREATER THINGS...

SO SHE WENT TO OXFORD TO BECOME A CHEMIST

AT LAST SHE REALISED POLITICS WAS HER CALLING

THINGS REALLY TOOK OFF WHEN SHE GOT A NEW NAME:
THATCHER

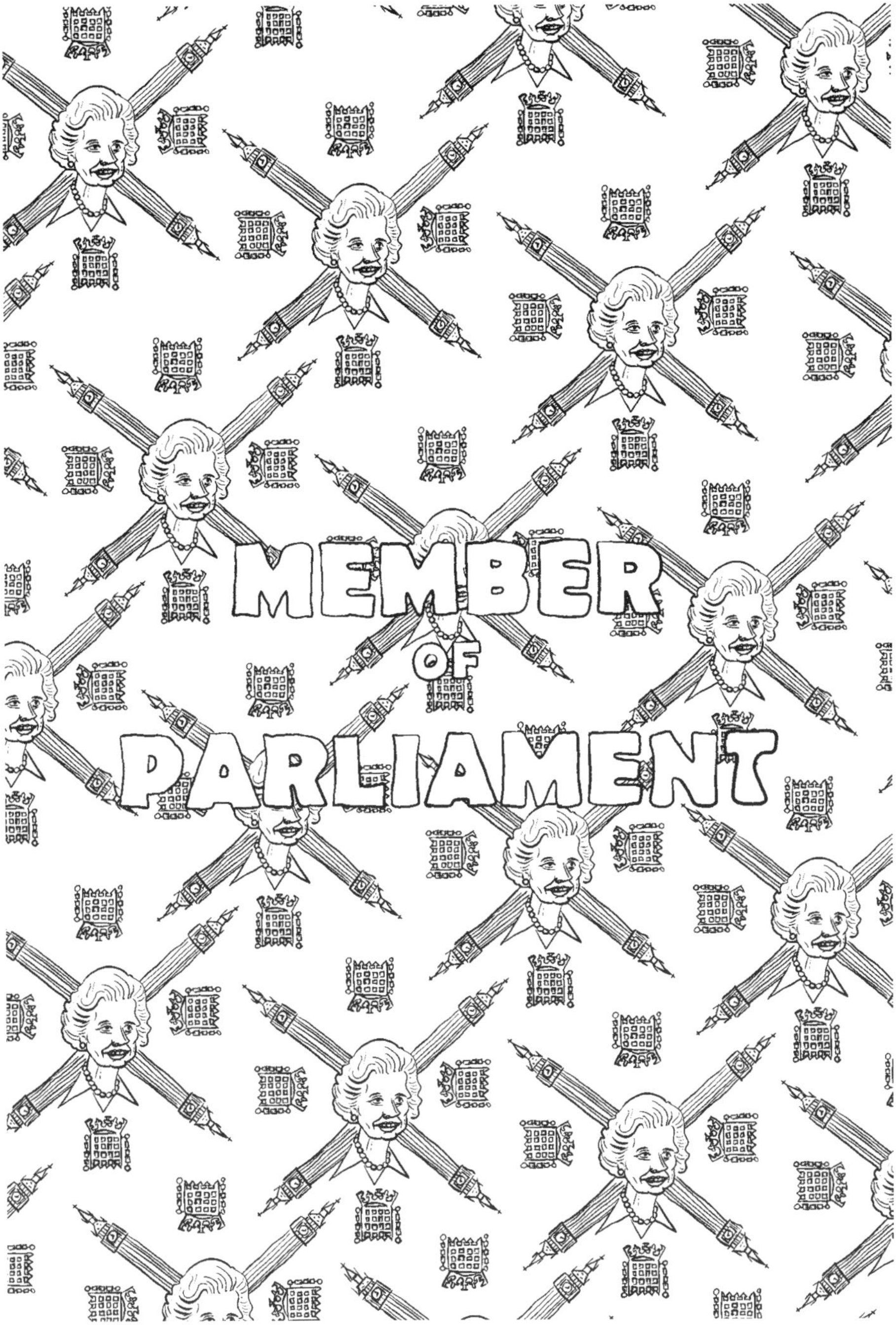
MEMBER
OF
PARLIAMENT

HER CHILDREN LOVED PLAYING WITH HER EXTENSIVE COLLECTION OF PEARLS

BUT HER POLITICAL REPUTATION SUFFERED A SETBACK
AFTER SHE WAS CAUGHT STEALING MILK

FORTUNATELY, TED HEATH WAS HER BIGGEST SUPPORTER.
HE PUT HER IN HIS CABINET.

AND HE WAS DELIGHTED TO STEP ASIDE
FOR HER TO BECOME LEADER

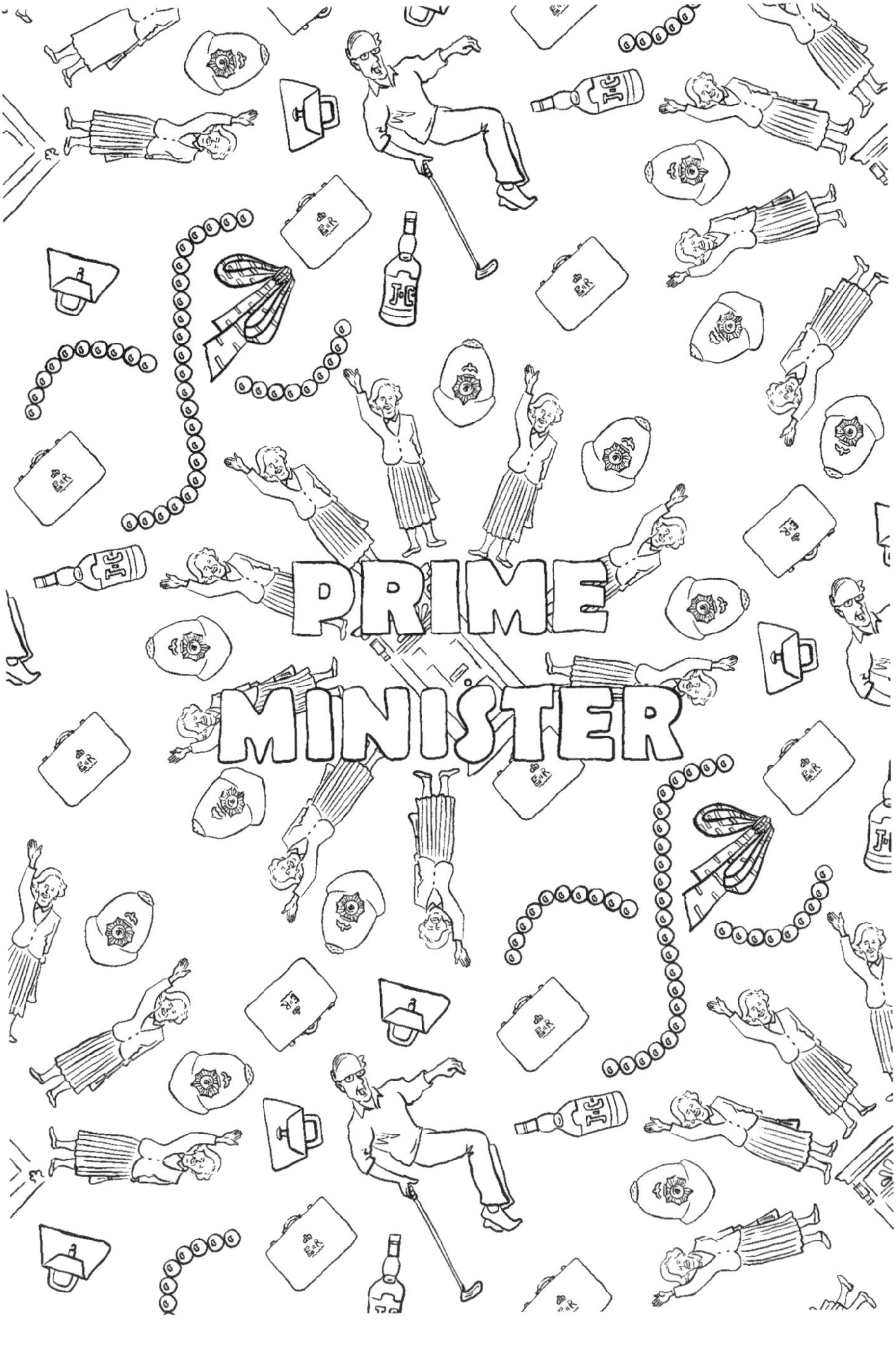
PRIME
MINISTER

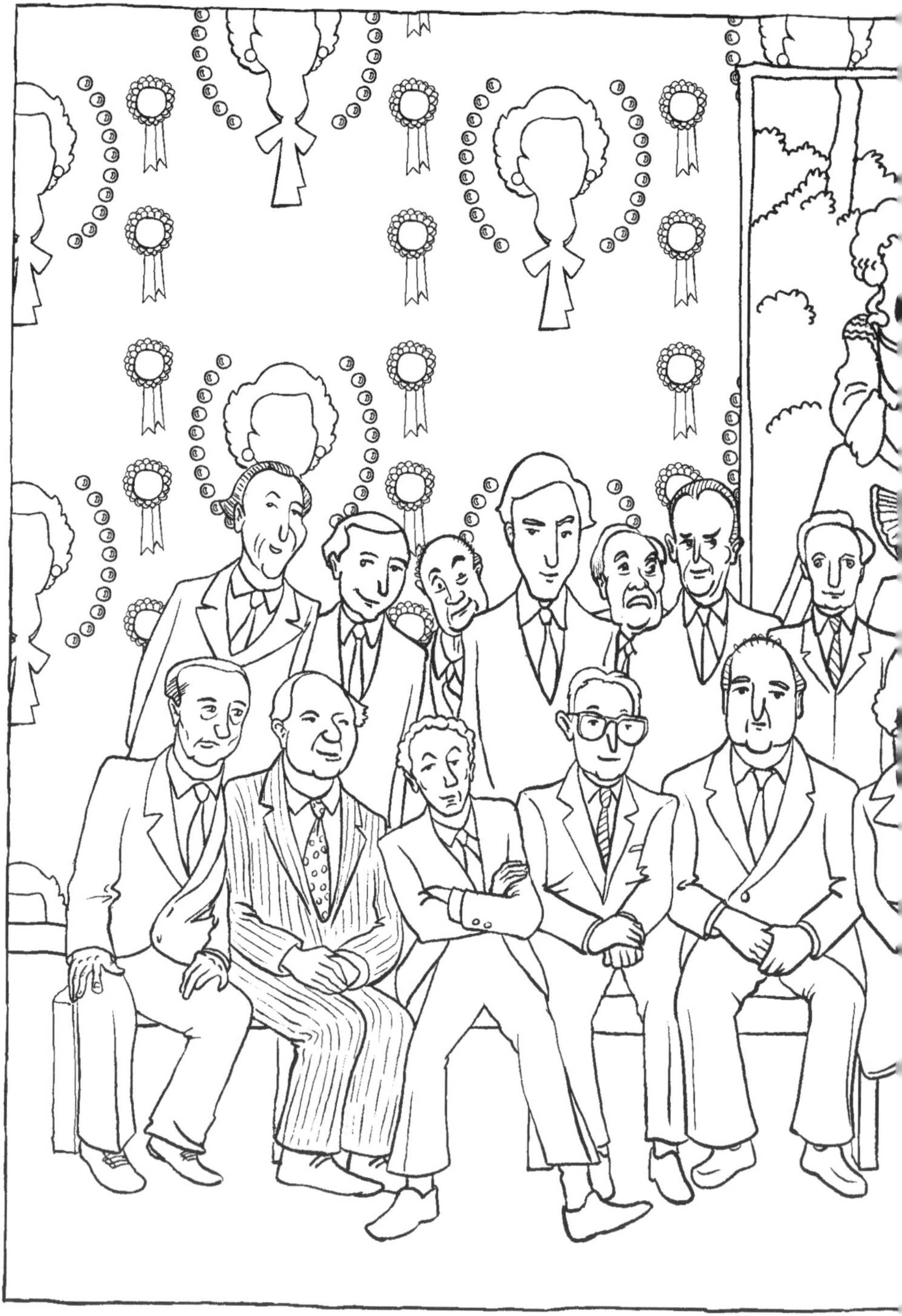

IN 1979, THATCHER ASSE

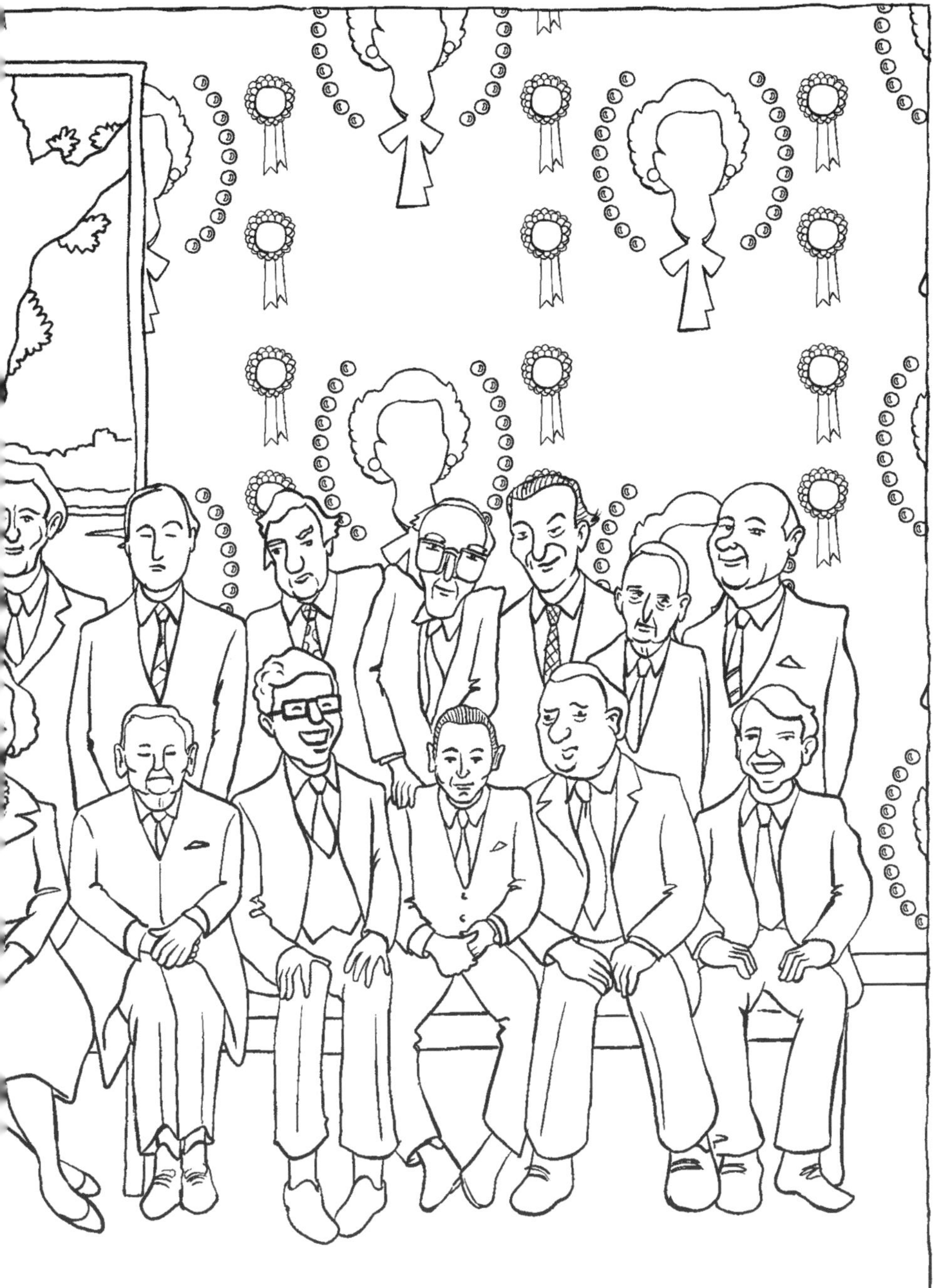

ED HER OWN CABINET

MARGARET'S WARDROBE: CUT OUT AND COLOUR

SHE WAS A BIG FAN OF THE UNION JACK

WINSTON CHURCHILL WAS HER OBI-WAN

SHE WASN'T SHY IN EXPRESSING HER FEELINGS

SHE WAS VERY PROUD OF HER IRON LADY IMAGE

ALTHOUGH SOMETIMES SHE COULD TAKE IT TOO FAR

AT NIGHT SHE DREAMT OF RIDING INTO BATTLE AGAINST COMMUNISM

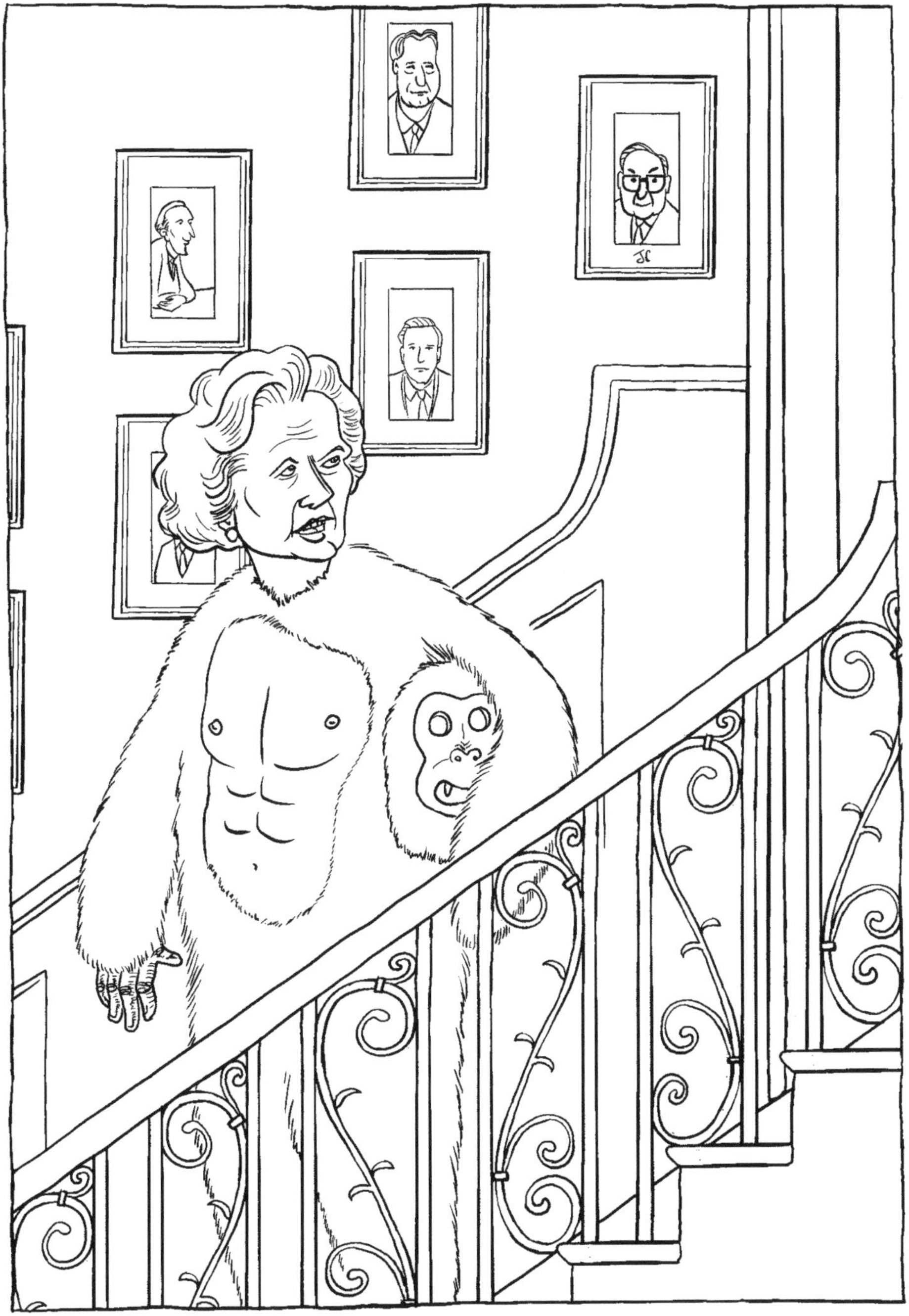

SHE LOVED FANCY DRESS

AND WAS A REGULAR GUEST AT THE WHITE HOUSE PARTIES

SHE WAS RESPONSIBLE FOR MAKING THE USA AND RUSSIA
THE GREAT FRIENDS THEY ARE TODAY

SHE WAS PRAISED FOR TACKLING ARGENTINA HEAD ON

AND HER DECISIVENESS IN SECURING PETER FALK'S LAND
WON HER RESPECT

EVEN IN THE MIDST OF GLOBAL CRISES, SHE AND DENIS NEVER
MISSED THEIR FAVOURITE PROGRAMME

SHE INSISTED ON HOLDING THE CONSERVATIVE PARTY CONFERENCES
FROM A BOAT

THATCHER CLOSED THE UK'S GOLD MINES, WHICH MADE THE
RICH NORTHERNERS VERY ANGRY

HISTORY WILL REMEMBER HER FOR
THE POLICY OF PRIVATE EYES IN UK INDUSTRY

HER INTENTION WAS TO TRANSFORM BRITAIN
INTO A NATION OF RICHARD BRANSONS

COLOUR IN YOUR FAVOURITE OF MAGGIE'S ALLIES

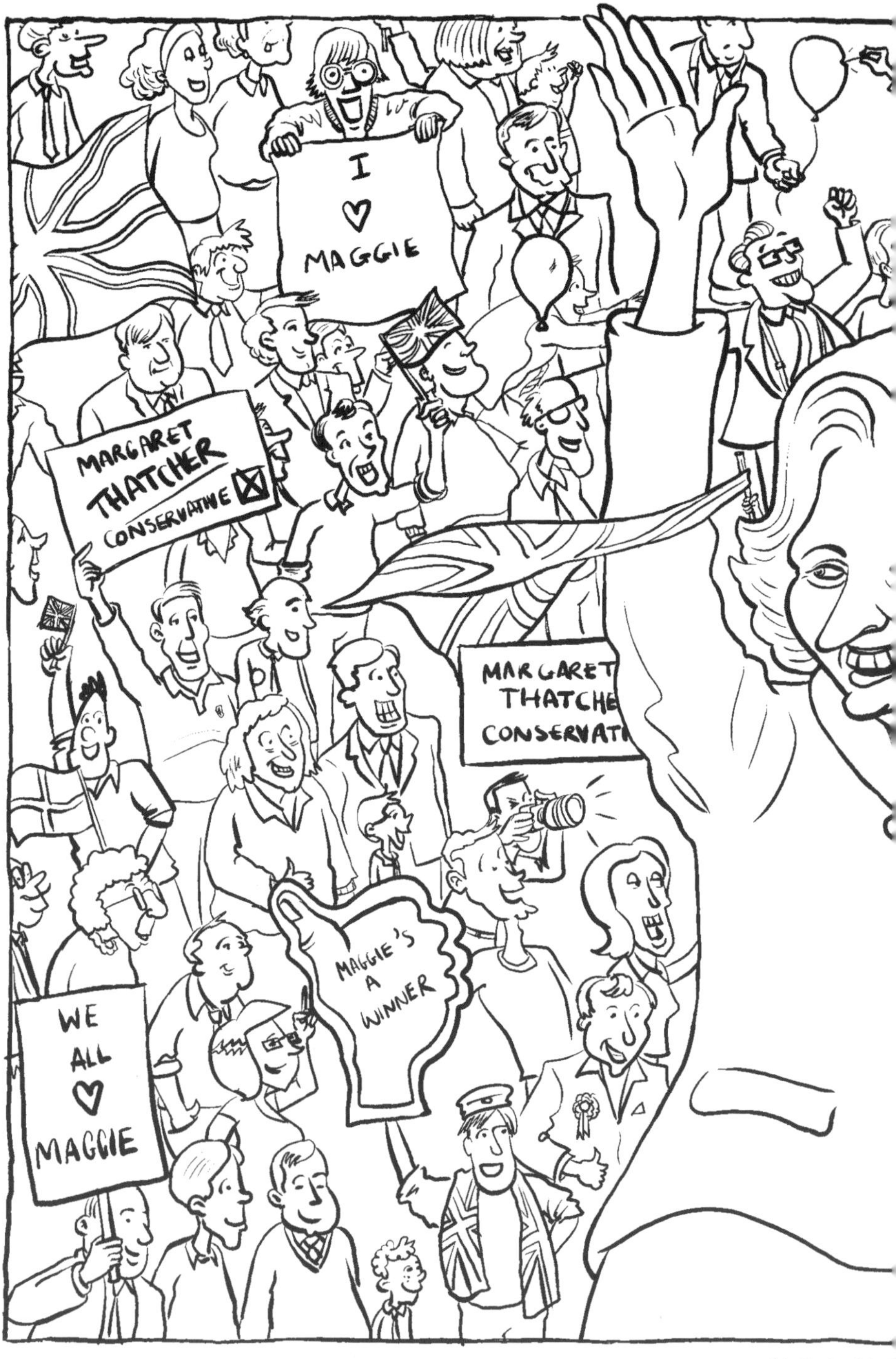
I ♥ MAGGIE
MARGARET THATCHER CONSERVATIVE
MARGARET THATCHE CONSERVATI
MAGGIE'S A WINNER
WE ALL ♥ MAGGIE

SHE DIVIDE

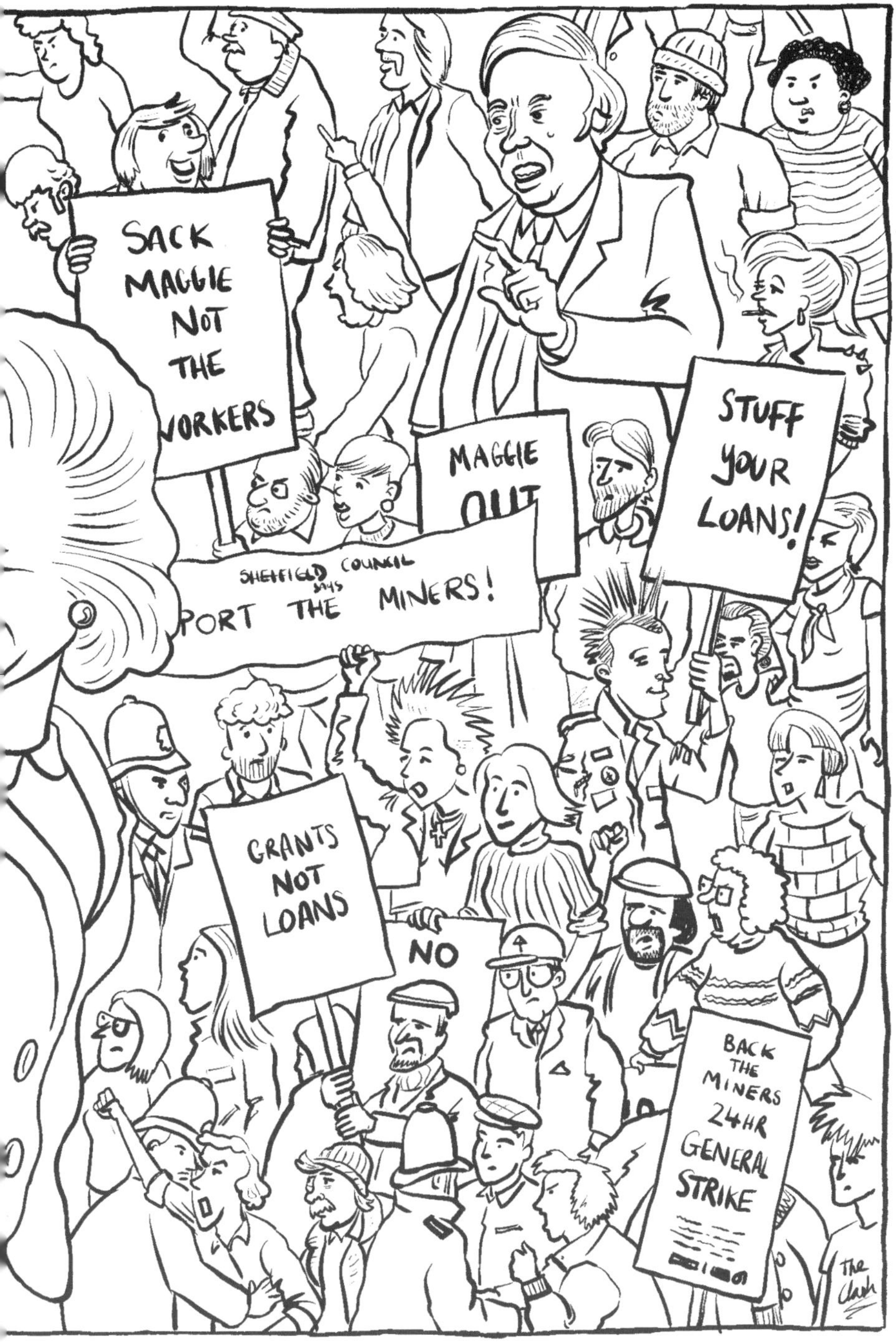
SACK MAGGIE NOT THE WORKERS
MAGGIE OUT
STUFF YOUR LOANS!
SHEFFIELD COUNCIL SAYS
PORT THE MINERS!
GRANTS NOT LOANS
NO
BACK THE MINERS 24HR GENERAL STRIKE
The Clash

THE NATION

UNTIL SHE FINALLY SUCCEEDED IN UNITING THE NATION - AGAINST HER

SHE WAS SWIFTLY BETRAYED BY HER OWN PARTY

HER FAREWELL SPEECH MOVED HER STAFF
(WHO WERE OUT OF JOBS) TO TEARS

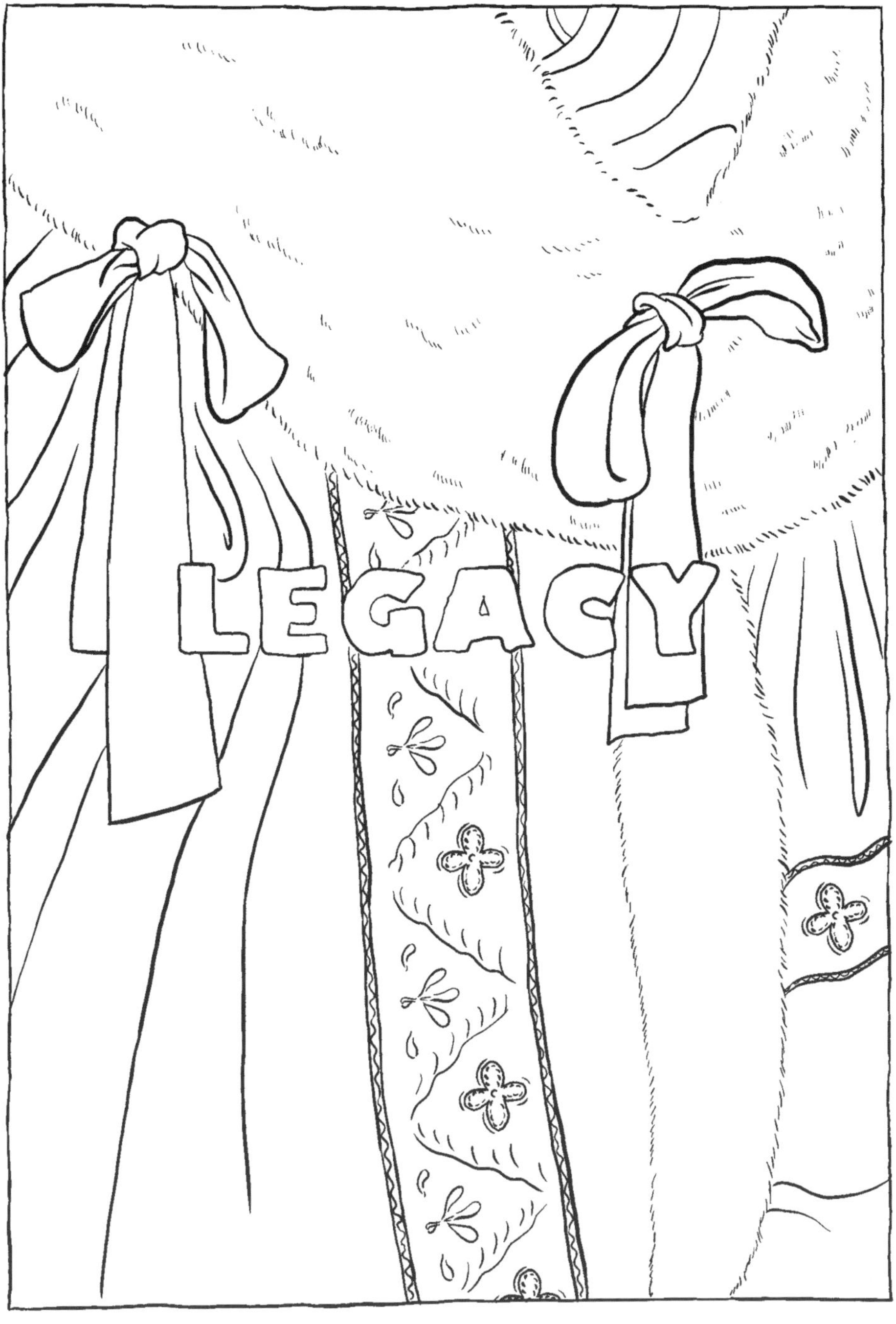
LEGACY

BUT THE DOOR TO No. 10 WAS ALWAYS OPEN TO HER

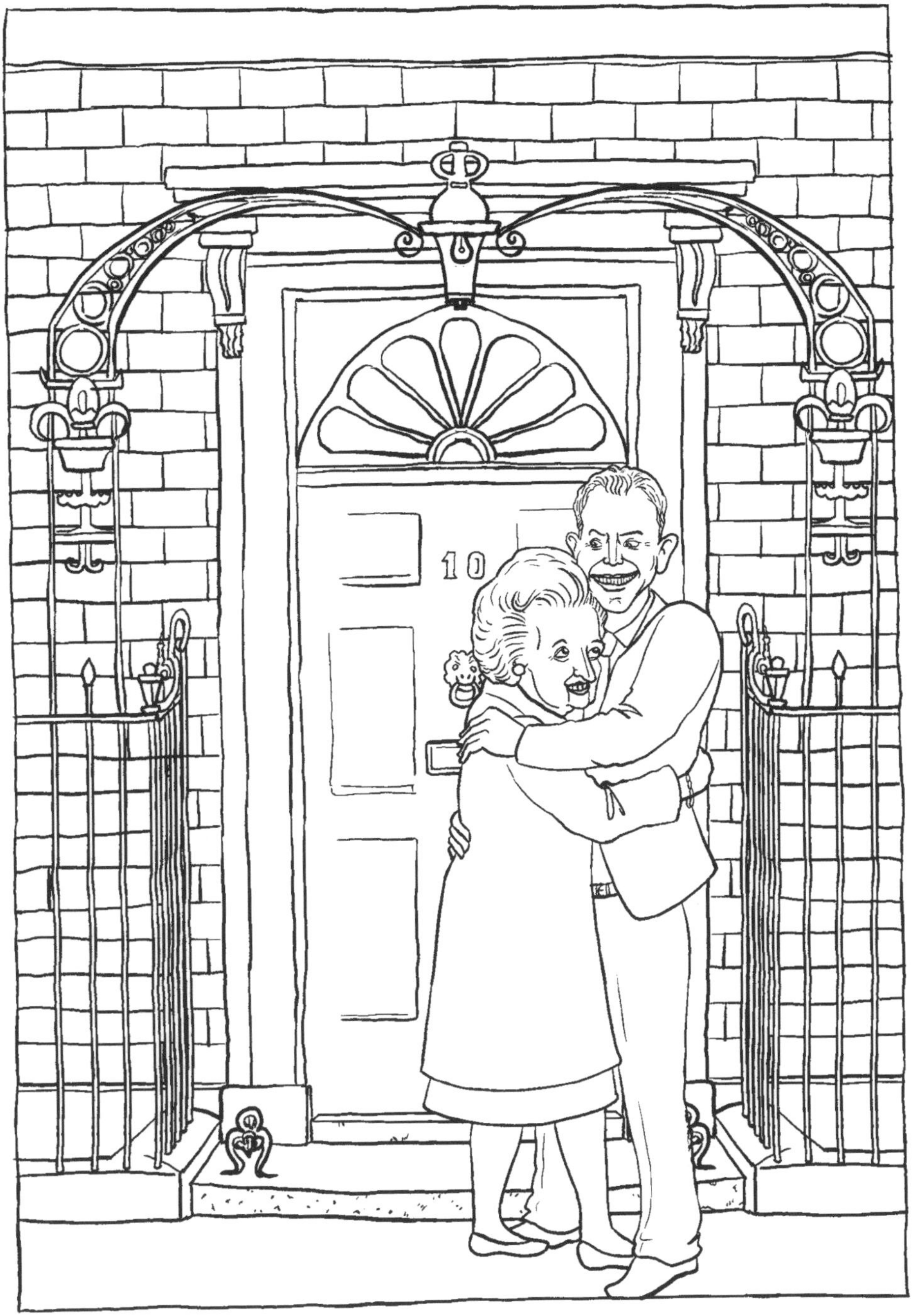
10

WHICH WAS FORTUNATE

BECAUSE SHE WAS ALWAYS DROPPING BY

...TRYING TO FIND THE CAPTAIN BEEFHEART LP SHE'D LEFT BEHIND IN 1990

EVEN IN HER OLD AGE, SHE STILL HELD THE PUBLIC'S INTEREST

HER FUNERAL WAS SO GRAND IT HAD ALL THE UNIFORMS

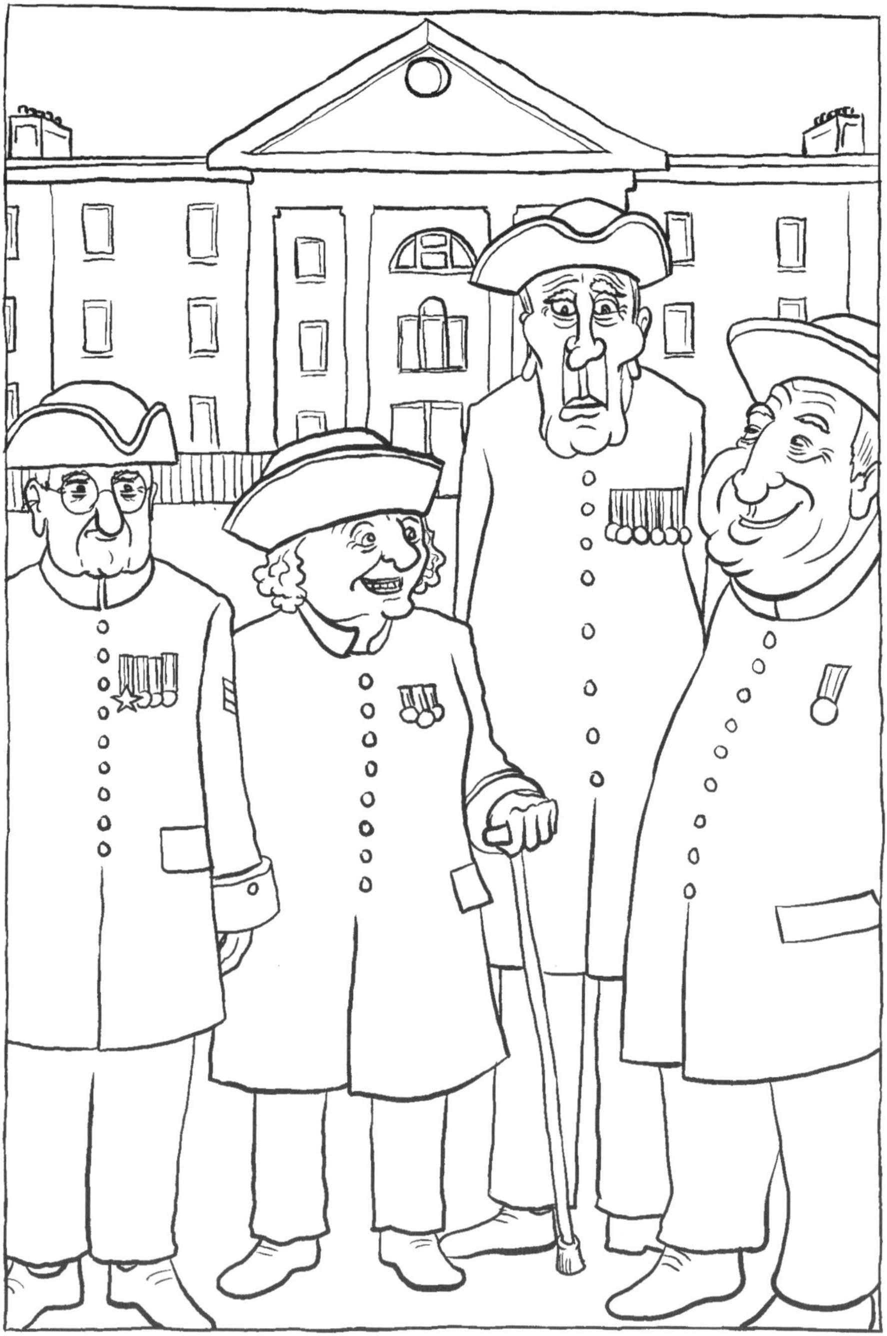

FOUR CHELSEA PENSIONERS WERE SPECIALLY CHOSEN TO BE BURIED ALIVE BESIDE HER

IN MADRID, A SQUARE HAS BEEN NAMED FOR HER, IN RECOGNITION
OF HER PASSION FOR FLAMENCO

HAD SHE BEEN ALIVE FOR BREXIT, SHE WOULD DEFINITELY HAVE
ADVOCATED LEAVING THE EU

HAD SHE BEEN ALIVE FOR BREXIT, SHE WOULD DEFINITELY HAVE ADVOCATED STAYING IN THE EU

POLITICIANS CONTINUE TO BE FASCINATED BY HER

THE THATCHER CELEBRITY GAUGE:
COLOUR IN WHERE YOU STAND

THE END